WEST VIRGINIA

The Mountain State

BY

JOHN HAMILTON

Abdo & Daughters

An imprint of Abdo Publishing | abdopublishing.com

abdopublishing.com

Published by ABDO Publishing, a division of ABDO, PO Box 398166, Minneapolis, Minnesota 55439. Copyright © 2017 by Abdo Consulting Group, Inc. International copyrights reserved in all countries. No part of this book may be reproduced in any form without written permission from the publisher. ABDO & Daughters™ is a trademark and logo of ABDO Publishing.

Printed in the United States of America, North Mankato, Minnesota.
082016
092016

Editor: Sue Hamilton   **Contributing Editor:** Bridget O'Brien
Graphic Design: Sue Hamilton
Cover Art Direction: Candice Keimig   **Cover Photo Selection:** Neil Klinepier
Cover Photo: iStock
Interior Images: Adventures on the Gorge, AP, Getty, Granger, Grave Creek Mound Archaeological Complex Museum, Gunter Küchler, History in Full Color-Restoration/Colorization, iStock, Jason Hollinger, John Brown Wax Museum, Library of Congress, Marshall University, Mile High Maps, Music in the Mountains Festival, National Park Service, One Mile Up, Steven Fox, Tim Kiser, Toyota Motor Manufacturing West Virginia, U.S. Air Force, U.S. National Archives/Lewis Hine, West Virginia University-Morgantown, and Wikimedia.

Statistics: *State and City Populations*, U.S. Census Bureau, July 1, 2015 estimates; *Land and Water Area*, U.S. Census Bureau, 2010 Census, MAF/TIGER database; *State Temperature Extremes*, NOAA National Climatic Data Center; *Climatology and Average Annual Precipitation*, NOAA National Climatic Data Center, 1980-2015 statewide averages; *State Highest and Lowest Points*, NOAA National Geodetic Survey.

Websites: To learn more about the United States, visit booklinks.abdopublishing.com. These links are routinely monitored and updated to provide the most current information available.

Cataloging-in-Publication Data

Names: Hamilton, John, 1959- author.
Title: West Virginia / by John Hamilton.
Description: Minneapolis, MN : Abdo Publishing, [2017] | Series: The United
    States of America | Includes index.
Identifiers: LCCN 2015957747 | ISBN 9781680783520 (lib. bdg.) |
    ISBN 9781680774566 (ebook)
Subjects: LCSH: West Virginia--Juvenile literature.
Classification: DDC 975.4--dc23
LC record available at http://lccn.loc.gov/2015957747

CONTENTS

THE MOUNTAIN STATE

West Virginia is nestled deep in the heart of the Appalachian Mountains. Residents and visitors alike love the state's breathtaking scenery. There are forested mountains, swift streams, deep gorges, and narrow valleys. Quaint small towns dot the countryside.

West Virginia is well known for its huge deposits of coal. It used to be called "the coal bin of the world." Most of today's coal is burned in power plants to produce electricity. The state doesn't mine as much coal as it once did, but it is still the nation's number-two supplier (behind Wyoming).

West Virginia got its name because it used to be part of the state of Virginia. During the Civil War (1861-1865), most residents of northwestern Virginia did not want to join the Southern Confederacy. The region broke away from Confederate Virginia. In 1863, it was admitted as a new state called West Virginia.

West Virginia is entirely within the region called the Appalachian Mountains. Because of the state's rugged peaks, it is nicknamed "The Mountain State."

The Appalachian Mountains near Snowshoe, West Virginia.

QUICK FACTS

Name: West Virginia separated from Virginia during the Civil War. It was admitted to the Union as a new state in 1863. Because it was on the west side of Virginia, it was named West Virginia.

State Capital: Charleston, population 49,736

Date of Statehood: June 20, 1863 (35th state)

Population: 1,844,128 (38th-most populous state)

Area (Total Land and Water): 24,230 square miles (62,755 sq km), 41st-largest state

Largest City: Charleston, population 49,736

Nickname: The Mountain State

Motto: *Montani semper liberi* (Mountaineers Are Always Free)

State Bird: Cardinal

State Flower: Rhododendron

State Gem/Fossil: Mississippian Fossil Coral

State Tree: Sugar Maple

State Songs: "West Virginia, My Home Sweet Home"; "The West Virginia Hills"; "This is My West Virginia"

Highest Point: Spruce Knob, 4,863 feet (1,482 m)

Lowest Point: Potomac River at Harpers Ferry, 240 feet (73 m)

Average July High Temperature: 83°F (28°C)

Record High Temperature: 112°F (44°C), in Martinsburg on July 10, 1936

Average January Low Temperature: 21°F (-6°C)

Record Low Temperature: -37°F (-38°C), in Lewisburg on December 30, 1917

Average Annual Precipitation: 46 inches (117 cm)

Number of U.S. Senators: 2

Number of U.S. Representatives: 3

U.S. Postal Service Abbreviation: WV

GEOGRAPHY

West Virginia is one of the smallest states in the nation. It covers just 24,230 square miles (62,755 sq km) of land and water. Only nine states are smaller. West Virginia shares borders with five states. Virginia is to the southeast. Maryland and Pennsylvania are to the northeast. Ohio borders the northwest, and Kentucky is to the southwest.

West Virginia is nicknamed "The Mountain State." It lies entirely within the Appalachian Mountains, a line of mountains that stretch from southeastern Canada to Alabama. The average elevation of West Virginia is about 1,500 feet (457 m), the highest of any state east of the Mississippi River.

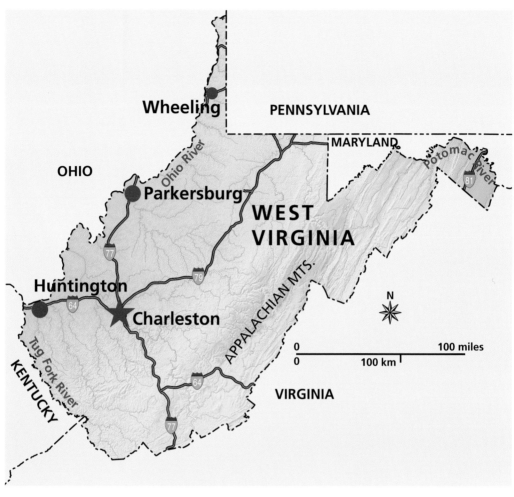

West Virginia's total land and water area is 24,230 square miles (62,755 sq km). It is the 41st-largest state. The state capital is Charleston.

The rugged Allegheny Mountains are part of the Appalachian Mountains. They stretch along the eastern side of West Virginia. The state's highest point is there. It is Spruce Knob, which rises to 4,863 feet (1,482 m).

Because there are a lot of mountains and steep valleys in West Virginia, roads must curl around narrow mountain passes. With so few large expanses of flat land, there are many small towns in the state. Also, the soil is mostly thin and rocky. There isn't as much farming in West Virginia as in some other states.

Harpers Ferry, West Virginia, is at the confluence of the Potomac and Shenandoah Rivers. West Virginia, Virginia, and Maryland all meet at this location. It is known as "The Point."

Shenandoah River

The Ohio River is West Virginia's most important river. It winds along much of the state's northwestern border with the state of Ohio. The Potomac River forms the northeastern border of West Virginia. The Tug Fork River forms much of the southwestern border.

There are no large natural lakes in West Virginia. Several artificial lakes have been formed by building dams on rivers. These artificial lakes include Bluestone Lake, East Lynn Lake, and Summersville Lake.

West Virginia has two panhandles. A panhandle is an area of land that juts out from the main section, like the handle of a frying pan. There is a northern panhandle that juts up between Pennsylvania and Ohio. There is another panhandle that juts out toward Maryland to the east.

Potomac River

CLIMATE AND
WEATHER

West Virginia has a humid subtropical climate. That means it has hot, humid summers, and cool winters. In the higher mountains, winters can be cold and snowy. The state's mountains can make the weather hard to predict. There can be different weather conditions even short distances apart because of the rapid changes in elevation.

Statewide, the average July high temperature is 83°F (28°C). The record high occurred on July 10, 1936, in the town of Martinsburg. On that day, the thermometer soared to 112°F (44°C).

The average January low temperature in West Virginia is 21°F (-6°C). The record low occurred in the town of Lewisburg on December 30, 1917. On that day, the temperature plunged to a teeth-chattering -37°F (-38°C).

Horses eat during a snowstorm in Beckley, West Virginia.

A rainbow forms after rain delayed a summer baseball game in Fairmont, West Virginia.

West Virginia receives about 46 inches (117 cm) of precipitation statewide each year. Snowfall varies greatly in winter because of the mountains. In the southwestern part of the state, 20 inches (51 cm) might fall. However, more than 64 inches (163 cm) might fall in the eastern mountains.

Tornadoes rarely whirl over West Virginia, and the state is too far inland to be struck directly by hurricanes. However, common summer thunderstorms can sometimes cause severe flooding.

PLANTS AND
ANIMALS

Forests cover nearly 78 percent of West Virginia's land area. That is about 12 million acres (4.9 million ha). Many kinds of trees grow in the state's forests. The most common trees are yellow poplar and white oak. Other trees include red maple, chestnut oak, northern red oak, hickory, beech, black cherry, white ash, Virginia pine, eastern hemlock, and white pine. Flowering trees include hawthorn, dogwood, and wild crab apple. The sugar maple is the official state tree of West Virginia.

In years past, invasive insect pests from other countries, such as gypsy moth caterpillars, destroyed many of West Virginia's trees, especially dogwoods, oaks, and firs. New state conservation programs are helping to fight the insects and restore the forests.

There are dozens of species of wildflowers that add splashes of color to West Virginia's forest floors and meadows. Common spring wildflowers include yellow fawn lily, marsh marigold, fire pink, stonecrop, common blue violet, columbine, bloodroot, chickweed, Indian paintbrush, and lousewort.

Marsh Marigold

Fire Pink

Common Blue Violet

Deciduous trees in a West Virginia forest.

Flying Squirrel

White-Tailed Deer

Before European settlers came to West Virginia, several species of large mammals roamed the mountain forests and valleys. They included America bison, elk, and gray wolves. Overhunting caused these animals to disappear from West Virginia. White-tailed deer, however, are common all over the state. Mountain lions are present but rarely sighted. Black bears are found high in wooded mountain areas.

Smaller mammals commonly found in West Virginia include red foxes, coyotes, raccoons, long-tailed weasels, eastern spotted skunks, bobcats, feral pigs, river otters, opossums, shrews, little brown bats, chipmunks, southern flying squirrels, and snowshoe hares.

Cardinal

With its mild climate, West Virginia is home to more than 300 species of birds. Commonly spotted soaring through the skies are blue jays, mourning doves, chickadees, sparrows, woodpeckers, crows, grackles, eastern bluebirds, purple martins, red-tailed hawks, bald eagles, starlings, mockingbirds, and black-throated blue warblers. The cardinal is West Virginia's official state bird. Male cardinals have a bright-red coloring and a loud, whistling song. Cardinals are yearlong residents of the state.

West Virginia has 178 species of fish that can be found swimming in the state's rivers, mountain lakes, and reservoirs. Common fish include northern pike, muskellunge, catfish, sucker, carp, white perch, striped bass, smallmouth and largemouth bass, crappie, cutthroat trout, rainbow trout, and brown trout. The official state fish of West Virginia is the brook trout.

Brook Trout

HISTORY

People have lived in the area of present-day West Virginia for at least 14,000 years, and perhaps longer. These Paleo-Indians were the early ancestors of today's Native Americans. They were nomads who hunted large animals such as mammoths and bison.

The Fort Ancient people were mound builders who lived in the area from about 1000 to 1650 AD. Little is known about these early peoples, but some of the large earthen mounds they built are still visible today. The mounds were probably used in religious ceremonies, such as burials.

Grave Creek Mound, at 69 feet (21 m) high and 295 feet (90 m) in diameter, is the largest cone-shaped burial mound in the United States.

As time passed, several Native American tribes developed. They settled or hunted in the West Virginia area. The tribes included the Moneton, Cherokee, Conoy, Delaware, and Shawnee people.

From 1775-1777, Shawnee Chief Cornstalk first fought, then tried to negotiate treaties between his people and settlers. He was killed by soldiers at Fort Randolph in West Virginia.

A pioneer cabin below the cliffs of Seneca, West Virginia. By the 1700s, many independent people in the west side of Virginia wanted to form their own state.

When Europeans claimed North America in the early 1600s, West Virginia was a part of Virginia. Rugged mountains kept most settlers out of West Virginia. There were also land disputes between the French, English, and Native Americans.

In the late 1700s, large numbers of people began moving into present-day West Virginia. They were often unhappy with the government of Virginia. These pioneers were usually poor, with an independent, frontier way of thinking. Many people in the west side of Virginia already wanted to form their own state.

The John Brown Wax Museum in Harpers Ferry shows Brown's failed 1859 revolt against slavery at the city's armory.

In 1859, an abolitionist named John Brown led a revolt against slavery. He and a group of men raided a government armory in Harpers Ferry, in today's West Virginia. Brown was captured, tried, and hanged. Although his plan failed, it inspired others to oppose slavery.

In 1861, the Civil War began. Slavery was a big reason why the North and South went to war. The Southern states had large plantations. They wanted slaves to work on those plantations. The Northern states wanted laws forbidding people to own slaves.

In 1861, the state of Virginia voted to secede, or leave, the United States. But people in the west side of Virginia wanted to stay in the Union. They did not like slavery. They voted to leave Virginia. More than 32,000 West Virginians fought for the Union during the Civil War. West Virginia officially became the 35th state in 1863.

In the 1870s, railroads expanded into West Virginia. This brought businesses into the state. It also helped miners get their coal to cities in other states.

In the early 1900s, there were problems between coal miners and the owners of the mines. The mines were often tragically unsafe. Many miners risked their lives every time they went to work. However, the owners did not want to negotiate with the workers. Disagreements between miners and owners sometimes led to violence.

Workers outside a mine in Brown, West Virginia, in 1908. Many miners worked in unsafe conditions. This caused arguments, and sometimes violence, between workers and mine owners.

A coal miner at home in Scott's Run, West Virginia, in 1937. Many West Virginia coal miners were out of work during the Great Depression. Even those who had jobs were often poor.

The Great Depression struck in 1929 and lasted throughout much of the 1930s. The bad economy caused many people to lose their jobs, homes, and businesses. West Virginia was hit very hard.

In 1941, the United States entered World War II (1939-1945). The war created a big demand for coal. The state's forests were also needed to supply timber for housing and other goods. Suddenly, people in West Virginia went back to work. The state's economy greatly improved.

Fostoria Glass Works, Moundsville, W. Va.

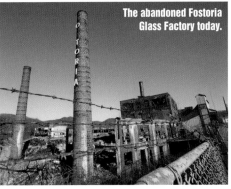

The abandoned Fostoria Glass Factory today.

The Fostoria Glass Company built its factory in Moundsville, West Virginia, in 1891. The company produced stemware, plates, lamps, and other glass items. It once employed more than 900 people. Fostoria was one of the largest manufacturers of handmade glass in the United States. In the 1970s, foreign competition brought a serious decline in sales. The factory closed in 1983.

After World War II, West Virginia's economy had its ups and downs. As technology improved, fewer miners were needed. Machines replaced people. Many miners lost their jobs. Factories suffered from foreign competition. Environmental damage from decades of poor mining techniques caused big problems.

In the past few decades, more people have found jobs. More high-tech companies have moved into the state. West Virginia continues to improve its environmental record. Tourism has become more important to the state's economy, as people travel to West Virginia to enjoy its spectacular natural beauty.

Today, many tourists come to enjoy West Virginia's natural beauty.

HISTORY

DID YOU KNOW?

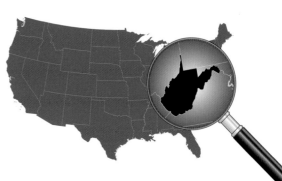

• Coal mining is West Virginia's best-known industry. Coal can be found in 53 of West Virginia's 55 counties. The state ranks second in the nation in coal mining (behind Wyoming). John Peter Salling and John Howard first discovered coal in West Virginia in 1742. In the early 1800s, people started burning it instead of wood in furnaces. Today, more than 90 percent of power plants used to generate electricity in West Virginia run on coal. Mining can be a very hazardous job. In 1907, 362 miners were killed in a coal dust explosion in the Monongah Mine. In January 2006, there was an explosion in the Sago Mine, which killed 12 miners. In 2010, at the Upper Big Branch Mine in Montcoal, 29 miners lost their lives. New government inspections and safety programs have helped make today's mines less hazardous, but there is still much danger.

A coal miner works next to a drill in an area that is only about 3.3 feet (1 m) tall. Many safety measures have been put into place, but mining is still dangerous.

• Bridge Day is one of the most popular extreme sports festivals in the world. It is held each October in Fayette County, West Virginia. BASE jumpers from all over the country take their turn leaping off the 876-foot (267-m) New River Gorge Bridge. The bridge is the second-longest single arch bridge in the United States. Bridge Day is the only day that people can legally jump from the span and parachute to the bottom of the gorge. Each year, about 80,000 people come to watch the daredevils in action.

PEOPLE

Charles "Chuck" Yeager (1923-) was a U.S. Air Force test pilot at a time when jet aircraft were first being flown. In 1947, he became the first person to fly faster than the speed of sound. Born in Myra, West Virginia, he started his career as an aircraft mechanic. After training to become a pilot, he flew dozens of combat missions during World War II (1939-1945). He became a test pilot after the war. New jet aircraft often crashed. Yeager kept his concentration even during extreme stress. After breaking the sound barrier with the Bell X-1, Yeager flight-tested many kinds of new jet aircraft. He rose to the rank of brigadier general. Yeager was definitely a test pilot who had "the right stuff."

Mary Lou Retton (1968-) was the first American athlete to win a gold medal in gymnastics. At the 1984 Summer Olympic Games in Los Angeles, California, she won five medals, including the all-around gold medal. During the all-around competition, she scored a perfect 10 on the vault, the final event, which put her in the lead by just .05 points. Her Olympic Games victories turned her into a major celebrity in the United States. Retton has also won many international competitions. In 1997, she was inducted into the International Gymnastics Hall of Fame. Retton was born in Fairmont, West Virginia.

Thomas "Stonewall" Jackson (1824–1863) was a Confederate general during the Civil War (1861-1865). He was born in Clarksburg, West Virginia. He fought in the Mexican-American War (1846-1848). When the Civil War began in 1861, he joined the Confederate Army of the Southern states. He earned his nickname "Stonewall" by holding back Union forces at the First Battle of Bull Run (also called the Battle of First Manassas). Jackson was an excellent war planner, and an inspiration to the South. Unfortunately for the Confederate Army, he was accidentally shot by his own men at the Battle of Chancellorsville and died soon afterward.

Don Knotts (1924–2006) was one of the most-beloved Hollywood actors of all time. He was born and grew up in Morgantown, West Virginia. He joined the United States Army during World War II (1939-1945). After the war, he graduated from West Virginia University. In the 1950s, he starred in several television shows, films, and stage productions. In the 1960s, Knotts took his most famous role, playing Barney Fife, the skinny, nervous deputy on *The Andy Griffith Show*. He earned five Emmy Awards for the role. Knots also played lovable Ralph Furley on the TV show *Three's Company*, and he starred in many movies, mostly comedies such as *The Apple Dumpling Gang* and *The Ghost and Mr. Chicken*.

CITIES

Charleston is the largest city in West Virginia. It is also the state capital. It is located in the west-central part of the state, where the Kanawha and Elk Rivers come together. Charleston was first settled in the late 1700s. As pioneers came west, many stopped at the village, and Charleston grew. It became the permanent state capital in 1885. Today, the city's population is about 49,736. The area around Charleston is rich in coal, oil, and natural gas. Top employers include businesses that make plastics, chemicals, and other products. The University of Charleston was founded in 1888. West Virginia State University is located nearby. Festivals are held each year in the city, including those that highlight local bluegrass music and Appalachian clog dancing.

Huntington is the second-largest city in West Virginia. Its population is about 48,638. It is located in the southwestern part of the state, along the Ohio River. The city was first settled in the late 1700s. It became an important railroad hub. The train traffic helped create, build, and grow the city's businesses. Today, Huntington is a center for high technology, health care, finance, and tourism. The city's factories make goods such as machinery, chemicals, and textiles. Marshall University enrolls more than 13,600 students. The Huntington Museum of Art is the state's largest art museum, featuring a large collection of blown glass, paintings, and sculptures. The Huntington Music & Arts Festival is held each September. It celebrates regional music, food, and arts.

Parkersburg is located along the Ohio River in the northwestern part of West Virginia. It is the state's third-largest city. Its population is about 30,991. The area was settled in the late 1700s, and was officially named Parkersburg in 1810. New railroads helped the city grow in the 1860s. Today, the city is a center for manufacturing and agriculture. Oil and natural gas are major industries. West Virginia University at Parkersburg enrolls more than 4,200 students. The Henry Cooper House is a restored two-story log cabin. It has exhibits that tell the story of the city's early pioneer days.

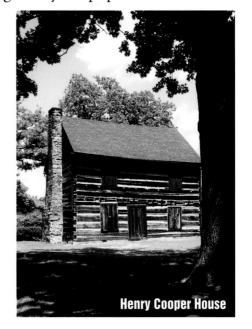

Henry Cooper House

Wheeling lies along the banks of the Ohio River in West Virginia's northern panhandle region. Its population is about 27,648. First settled in 1769 as a rugged frontier town, Wheeling today has many different kinds of businesses, from natural gas and oil processing to high-tech research and service industries. There are many historic buildings in downtown, including West Virginia Independence Hall, the place where the people of West Virginia voted to break away from Confederate Virginia and form their own state. Jamboree in the Hills is an annual summer festival held near Wheeling. Thousands of country music fans gather at the four-day festival to see some of the top acts in the nation perform on stage.

West Virginia Independence Hall

TRANSPORTATION

For much of West Virginia's history, the state's rugged terrain made travel difficult. Tunnels and bridges have improved the transportation system, but highways still must wind around many steep mountains and valleys.

West Virginia has 38,750 miles (62,362 km) of public roadways. Interstate I-77 travels north and south across the western part of the state, passing through Parkersburg and the capital city of Charleston. Interstate I-64 winds mostly east and west. It also passes through Charleston. Interstate I-79 begins in Charleston and travels to the northeast, passing through Morgantown before exiting into Pennsylvania.

The New River Gorge Bridge is a steel arch bridge over the New River Gorge near Fayetteville, West Virginia. It is 3,030 feet (924 m) long, and is used by about 16,000 vehicles each day.

A passenger train moves through a tunnel near the Harpers Ferry Train Station.

There are eight freight railroads in West Virginia operating on 2,226 miles (3,582 km) of track. The most common product hauled by train is coal. Other products include chemicals, metal products, plus sand and gravel. Amtrak's Cardinal line whisks passengers east and west across the southern part of the state, passing through Charleston, Hinton, and several other cities.

Large barges haul bulky goods up and down rivers in the western part of the state, especially on the Ohio River. The busiest ports are located in Huntington and Parkersburg.

West Virginia has five main commercial airports. The busiest is Yeager Airport, near Charleston. It handles about 500,000 passengers each year.

NATURAL RESOURCES

West Virginia was once known as the "coal bin of the world." Coal continues to be one of the state's most important natural resources, although mining has declined in recent years. Coal is found in 53 of 55 West Virginia counties. The state is a major producer, second only to Wyoming. Oil and natural gas deposits are also mined in the western and central parts of the state. Other products mined from the Earth include clay, limestone, plus sand and gravel.

West Virginia contains 12 million acres (4.9 million ha) of forestland. That is about 78 percent of the state's total area. Logging on commercial forestland is big business in West Virginia. Hardwoods such as yellow poplars, oaks, and maples are harvested to make many products, including furniture, building products, and shingles for roofs.

Coal is one of West Virginia's most important natural resources.

Hay is harvested and stacked at a farm near Teays Valley, West Virginia.

Farming is not as big an industry in West Virginia as in other states. There are too many mountains and steep valleys for large agricultural operations. There are about 20,900 farms in the state. Most are small, with an average size of just 172 acres (70 ha). The most valuable crops raised include hay, corn, and soybeans. Broiler chickens, turkeys, and chicken eggs are also produced. Valuable apples and peaches are grown in the eastern panhandle region. The golden delicious apple was famously discovered in the state in 1912. It is the official state apple.

Golden Delicious Apple

NATURAL RESOURCES

INDUSTRY

In times past, coal mining and logging were West Virginia's top industries. That changed in recent decades. Many power plants across the country have shifted to burning cheaper and cleaner natural gas. Also, new machinery has reduced the number of workers needed in West Virginia's coal mines. By relying so much on mining and just a few other industries, the whole state suffers during economic downturns.

West Virginia has made a big effort to diversify its economy by attracting different kinds of businesses to the state. In recent years, companies that manufacture chemicals and biotechnology products have come to West Virginia. Also settling in the state are firms that produce renewable energy products. Aerospace, telecommunications, automobiles, and health care are also growing.

Toyota Motor Manufacturing West Virginia employees cheer as the division produces a finished product from the company's second automatic transmission assembly line.

Above: The FBI's Criminal Justice Information Services (CJIS) Division building at Clarksburg, West Virginia. Left: A CJIS employee works on fingerprint identification.

Several government agencies have moved to West Virginia. They include the FBI's Criminal Justice Information Services Division, which gathers records on criminals, including computerized fingerprint identification.

Tourism has become very important to West Virginia's economy in recent years. People are attracted to the state's scenic beauty, quaint small towns, and outdoor activities. Each year, visitors spend nearly $5 billion in the state, enough to support 46,000 jobs.

SPORTS

There are no professional major league sports teams in West Virginia. There are minor league teams that play sports such as football, baseball, basketball, and hockey. High school and college sports are closely followed. The state has two colleges that play in National Collegiate Athletic Association (NCAA) Division I sports, the highest level of competition.

West Virginia University's main campus is in Morgantown. Its sports teams are called the Mountaineers. There are 17 men's and women's varsity teams. Football and basketball are especially popular. Marshall University is in Huntington. Its sports teams are called the Thundering Herd. Its football team is usually a tough contender. It was the inspiration for the hit 2006 film *We Are Marshall*.

Mountaineer is the mascot for West Virginia University in Morgantown.

Marco is the mascot for Marshall University in Huntington.

Whitewater rafting is a popular sport on the New River. The Upper River Gorge is calmer, while the Lower River Gorge has wilder rapids.

There are many outdoor sports opportunities in West Virginia's rugged wilderness. The mountains and valleys are great places for camping, hiking, caving, and backpacking. Whitewater rafters flock to the New River in southern West Virginia, anxious to test its wild, frothy rapids.

Many abandoned railways in the state have been turned into bicycling and hiking paths, which has boosted tourism. Fishing, hunting, and horseback riding are also popular. In winter, many people enjoy skiing, sledding, and ice skating.

SPORTS

ENTERTAINMENT

In the 1700s, during West Virginia's pioneer days, the mountains made travel difficult. People learned to rely on themselves for entertainment. Their music and crafts have been handed down for generations. Many people enjoy keeping the old traditions alive by playing in festivals and exhibiting artwork. Much of the traditional mountain folk music relies on the fiddle, also known as the violin. Young people and old-timers alike love to "cut a rug" by clog dancing to bluegrass music, accompanied by a fiddle and banjo.

Music in the Mountains Bluegrass Festival is a huge gathering of bluegrass music fans. It takes place each summer in the town of Summersville, West Virginia. Over four days, there are dozens of acts featuring some of the finest musicians from the region. Other music festivals in the state include the Appalachian String Band Music Festival in Clifftop, and the West Virginia State Folk Festival in Glenville.

Music in the Mountains Bluegrass Festival takes place each summer in Summersville, West Virginia.

Reenactors portray Civil War soldiers at Harpers Ferry National Historical Park.

There are many beautiful and historic places to visit in West Virginia. One of the most popular Civil War-era sites is Harpers Ferry National Historical Park. It is located in the city of Harpers Ferry, West Virginia, where the Potomac and Shenandoah Rivers meet. The historic site is where John Brown made his doomed abolitionist raid against the federal armory in 1859. The park includes historical buildings, Civil War exhibits, reenactments, and hiking trails.

ENTERTAINMENT

TIMELINE

12,000 BC—Paleo-Indians arrive in the present-day West Virginia area.

1600s—Moneton, Cherokee, Conoy, Delaware, and Shawnee Native Americans hunted in the West Virginia area.

Early 1700s—European settlers begin to filter into the area.

1742—Coal is discovered in West Virginia by John Peter Salling and John Howard.

1861—The Civil War begins. Virginia leaves the Union to join the Confederacy. The people of West Virginia declare themselves a separate state and ask to join the Union instead.

1863—West Virginia officially becomes the 35th state in the Union.

1870s—Many railroads are built across West Virginia.

1907—The Monongah Mine explosion kills 362 miners.

1917—The United States enters World War I. West Virginia sends troops to the war.

1929—The Great Depression begins. Many West Virginians lose their jobs, homes, and businesses.

1941—America enters World War II. West Virginia sends troops to the war. The state's natural resources are in demand, and the economy improves.

2010—The Upper Big Branch Mine explodes, killing 29 miners. New mine safety inspections and regulations are put in place.

2015—The West Virginia University Mountaineers women's soccer team wins its fourth consecutive regular-season Big 12 Conference championship.

GLOSSARY

ABOLITIONIST

A person who wants to end the practice of slavery. During and prior to the Civil War, many people, especially in Northern states, were abolitionists.

BASE JUMPING

Parachuting or wingsuit flying off a tall structure, such as a bridge, or a cliff. BASE stands for the kinds of tall objects that can be jumped from: **B**uilding, **A**ntenna, **S**pan, and **E**arth. Antenna usually refers to a tall radio or television antenna. Span means a bridge.

CIVIL WAR

The war fought between America's Northern and Southern states from 1861-1865. The Southern states were for slavery. They wanted to start their own country. Northern states fought against slavery and a division of the country.

CLOG DANCING

A type of folk dancing in which stiff shoes are used to strike heels and toes in a rhythmic way against the floor, or against each other. The most traditional shoes are wooden-soled clogs. Clog dancing is sometimes called flatfooting, or heel-and-toe dancing.

COAL

A rock that burns and is mined from underground. It is a fossil fuel that can be burned in power plants to turn turbines, which generate electricity.

Great Depression

A time of worldwide economic hardship beginning in 1929. Many people lost their jobs and had little money. The Great Depression finally eased in the mid-1930s, but didn't end until many countries entered World War II, around 1939.

Nomads

People who don't live in one place. Nomads are constantly traveling, usually following animal herds, which they hunt for food.

Panhandle

An area of land jutting out from the main part of the state, like the handle of a pan. West Virginia has two panhandles, one to the north, and one to the east.

Plantation

A large piece of land in which crops, like cotton, coffee, or tobacco, are raised and harvested by workers who live there. Many Southern plantations before the Civil War used African slaves as laborers.

Speed of Sound

The speed of sound waves traveling through air is about 700 miles per hour (1,127 km/hr) at 43,000 feet (13,106 m), the approximate altitude in which test pilot Chuck Yeager made his historic flight in 1947.

World War II

A conflict that was fought from 1939 to 1945, involving countries around the world. The United States entered the war after Japan bombed the American naval base at Pearl Harbor, in Oahu, Hawaii, on December 7, 1941.

INDEX